故園舊憶

庚寅中秋

韩启德题

故园画忆系列
Memory of the Old
Home in Sketches

老宁波遗风
Legacy of Old Ningbo

罗 枫 绘画
杨古城 撰文

Sketches by Luo Feng
Notes by Yang Gucheng

學苑出版社
Academy Press

图书在版编目（CIP）数据

老宁波遗风 / 杨古城撰文 ；罗枫绘. —北京 ：学苑出版社，2013.10

（故园画忆系列）

ISBN 978-7-5077-4403-3

Ⅰ. ①老… Ⅱ. ①杨… ②罗… Ⅲ. ①风俗习惯－宁波市－画册 Ⅳ. ①K892.455.3-64

中国版本图书馆CIP数据核字（2013）第242508号

出 版 人；孟 白
责任编辑：张 翔
出版发行：学苑出版社
地　　址：北京市丰台区南方庄2号院1号楼
电　　话：010-67675512　67678944　67601101（邮购）
邮　　编：100079
网　　址：www.book001.com
电子邮箱：xueyuan@public.bta.net.cn
经　　销：全国新华书店
印　　刷：北京彩蝶印刷有限公司
开　　本：889×1194　1/24
印　　张：5.5
版　　次：2013年11月第1版
印　　次：2013年11月第1次印刷
印　　数：3000册
定　　价：38.00元

筆畫老寧波

曹厚德題

序

宁波地处东南沿海，是7000年河姆渡史前文化发祥地、“海上丝绸之路”东方始发港和中国大运河最南端出海口，1986年12月被国务院公布为国家历史文化名城。港口城市海纳百川的气度和江南水乡水木清华的灵秀，使宁波这座城市充满张力而又深邃内敛。类型多元、底蕴丰厚的文化遗产资源，是宁波最可宝贵的精神财富。

作为一个地地道道的宁波人，我深爱这片土地的山山水水、一草一木。作为一个宁波文化工作者，我尤其酷爱老宁波的传统文化。第一次捧起《老宁波遗风》就忍不住一口气把它看完，老宁波的那一条条街道、一家家商铺、一间间房子、一座座小桥、一个个人物、一道道美食……在罗枫先生的笔之下跃然纸上、扑面而来，让人目不暇接、爱不释手。再细细品之，又深感时隔不久，罗枫先生的钢笔画更见功力，精确的人物造型、细致入微的描写，艺术地再现了老宁波的历史场景和生活印迹，让人为之惊叹、为之感动！

罗枫先生也是生于宁波、长于宁波，对宁波的历史和文化颇有研究，尤其在剪纸、绘画等众多领域有很深的造诣。我与先生相识相交多年，深知先生爱乡爱家之情，也对先生多年来坚持为家乡笔耕不辍钦佩有加。

面对城市化进程中老宁波、尤其是老宁波文化的逐步消失，留住城市文化遗存，守护共有精神家园，成为每一个宁波人义不容辞的责任。真诚祝愿罗枫先生文思泉涌、佳作叠出，真诚期盼有更多的“罗枫”一起加入宁波文化遗产保护行动、加入宁波文化强市建设大军，让宁波这座历史文化名城焕发新的活力和新的魅力！

是为序。

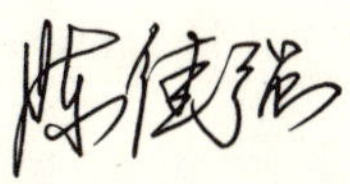

宁波市文化广电新闻出版局局长

2013年2月4日立春于宁波

Preface

Located on the southeast coast, Ningbo, the cradle of the 7,000-year old prehistoric Hemudu Culture, is the port of departure in the east for "Maritime Silk Road" and the southernmost estuary of the Grand Canal of China. It was declared a National Historical and Cultural City by the State Council in December 1986. Because of its location on the coast and south of the Yangtze river, the scenery is diverse and engaging and helps make the culture there more open, sophisticated and profound.. This diverse, rich cultural heritage is a precious intangible wealth of Ningbo.

I, a native of Ningbo, love everything about this place. As a cultural worker in Ningbo, I am particularly fond of its traditional culture. I read the entire *Legacy of Old Ningbo* without stop as soon as I got it. The streets, shops, houses, bridges, figures and cuisine of Ningbo are presented so vividly by the artistic pen of Mr. Luo Feng. Reading and viewing page after page, you are unable to put the book down until you have read and seen them all. Reading it again, I am astonished by the great contribution Mr. Luo Feng's pen drawings made to the value of the book. The precise drawings and subtle verbal descriptions have reproduced the historical scenes and existing traces of old Ningbo in an impressive artistic manner. How amazed and touched I am when reading this book!

Mr. Luo Feng was also born and grew up in Ningbo; so, he has studied the history and culture of Ningbo well, and developed a deep understanding on paper-cutting, drawing and many other artistic endeavors. We've been friends for years and I know the deep affection Mr. Luo Feng has for his hometown. I greatly appreciate his recreations of our hometown.

It is the bounden duty for every Ningbo citizen to value the cultural legacy and guard our old Ningbo spiritual home in the face of the urbanization process, especially as, in some cases, old Ningbo gradually disappears. I sincerely wish Mr. Luo Feng endless inspiration and creativity and earnestly look forward to more people follow his example and join in the protection for Ningbo cultural heritage and join the others as they work not only to protect but also enhance and make outsiders better know the cultural vigor and charm of old Ningbo!

Therefore, I happily write this Preface!

Chen Jiaqiang
Director, Ningbo Municipal Bureau of Culture,
Radio, TV, Film, Press and Publication
February 4, 2013 Ningbo

目　录

Contents

港湾·街巷

Harbors and Streets

宁波入海口

1832 年，英国东印度公司的林赛三次来华寻找良港，看中宁波。在广州谈判，签订《南京条约》时，强烈要求开放宁波作为通商口岸。

画中远景是镇海招宝山，占画面主要位置的大船都是当年的海运木船，桅杆如林。

Ningbo Estuary

In 1832, Hugh Hamilton Lindsay from the British East India Company visited China three times to look for a suitable harbor; he eventually chose Ningbo. Negotiating in Guangzhou under the "Treaty of Nanking", he strongly requested opening Ningbo as a trading port.

The distant mountain in the painting is Zhaobao Mountain in Zhenhai District; many masts of the wooden ships, essential for maritime transport at the time, dominate the scene..

江厦海运码头

宁波是唐宋以来中国“海上丝绸之路”对外开放的核心港口，江厦码头上停泊着与日本、朝鲜、爪哇、越南、泰国之间频繁往来的商船。古时江厦街的滨江处称“甬江码头”，俗称大道头，自古对外贸易热闹非凡，也是海鲜鱼货的集散地。

Jiangxia Ocean Wharf

Ever since the Tang and Song Dynasties (619-1127), Ningbo was an important port for the “Maritime Silk Road” of China. Merchant ships from Japan, Korea, Java, Vietnam, and Thailand frequently docked at Jiangxia Wharf. In ancient times the river bank at Jiangxia Street was called “Yongjiang Wharf”, also known as “End of Avenue”; it was a bustling site for foreign trade and a distribution center for seafood.

造船修船

古老的宁波港，是我国最早对外文明交流的窗口，也是世界舟楫文明的发源地之一。河网纵横而又滨海的宁波，有兴盛的造船修船的行业。

Shipbuilding and Repair

Ancient Ningbo Harbor was the earliest window for maritime civilization exchange with foreign countries in China, as well as one of the origins for the Chinese ship culture. Ningbo, with intersecting rivers and coastline, developed a flourishing shipbuilding and repair industry.

轮船码头

直到 20 年前，宁波人乘得最多的还是宁波开往上海的轮船，上下三层，每天或隔天一班，第一天傍晚从宁波外滩出发，第二天就可到达上海十六铺。画中的风景如今见不到了。

Ferry

Ningbo citizens mostly went to Shanghai by ferry until late 1900. The 3-deck ferry set off to Shanghai's Shillupu at dusk and arrived there the next morning. The scene depicted here can no longer be seen in Ningbo.

电力公司

1914年创办的宁波永耀电力公司发电厂厂址在北门外北斗河畔，对面是华美医院。民国时期它是宁波一家重要的大企业。现在遗留的部分建筑已列为“近代工业遗产”。

Electric Company

The Ningbo Yongyao Electric Company power plant established in 1914 was located on the bank of Beidou River outside Ningbo's North Gate opposite Huamei Hospital. The power plant was an important enterprise during the Republic of China, but now the remaining building is a part of Ningbo "Modern Industrial Heritage".

江亚轮海难

江亚轮是一艘由日本于 1939 年建造的中国轮船。归属宁波招商局，运营上海到宁波的海上航线。1948 年 12 月 3 日因爆炸沉没，整艘江亚轮仅 900 多人获救。招商局派出潜水员前往失事海域，打捞到尸体 1000 多具，罹难人数估计超过 3000 人，其中主要为宁波人。此次海滩成为 20 世纪中国最大的海难。此后，该船残体打捞后经过修复，于 1959 年重新投入运营，1966 年更名为东方红 8 号，1983 年退役。

JIANGYALUN Shipwreck

The JIANGYALUN was a Chinese ship built by the Japanese in 1939. It was owned by the Ningbo Merchants Bureau and plied the sea lane from Shanghai to Ningbo.

On 3 December 1948, the ship exploded and sank; only some 900 people were rescued. The Merchants Bureau sent divers to recover more than 1,000 bodies. It was estimated that more than 3,000 people died - mostly Ningbo citizens. It was the worst shipwreck in China in the 20th century.

In 1959 the ship was salvaged, restored, and resumed operation and renamed "Dong Fang Hong (The East is Red) No. 8" in 1966. It was retired from service in 1983.

江北天主教堂

天主教堂位于宁波市江北区中马路 40 号，由浙江教区的法籍苏主教兴建。清光绪二十五年（1899 年）增建钟楼。整座钟楼（包括琴室），由大堂、主教公署、本堂区及寝室、更衣室、藏书楼、慈母堂、印书房等组成，建筑面积有 4846.4 平方米。教堂钟楼是哥特式风格，保存完好。2006 年 6 月被国务院公布为全国重点文物保护单位。

Jiangbei Catholic Church

Located at No. 40 Zhongma Road, Jiangbei District, Ningbo, the Catholic Church was built by French Bishop Su who administered the Zhejiang Religious Region at that time. In 1899, a bell tower was built, which was composed of a hall, Mother Church sanctuary, Bishop's office and living quarters, library, piano room and printing house. The Gothic bell tower, with a floor area of 4,846.4m2, has been well preserved and declared a "National Key Cultural Relics Protection Unit" in June 2006 by the State Council.

海关缉私船

1684 年，清政府驰海禁，在宁波设立浙海关，为当时中国四大海关之一。鸦片战争后，宁波被列为五大通商口岸之一。1844 年正式开埠，英、法、美即来宁波设领事馆。清政府就在江北岸中马路设立海关税务司，对外征税，俗称海关。

1940 年 7 月，日军占镇海，欲进攻宁波，当夜宁波城防司令部向浙海关急调两艘巡辑舰，截巨石沉于航道，以阻日军进攻。

Anti-smuggling Ship of Customs

In 1684 the Qing Government boycotted marine transportation and established Zhejiang Customs in Ningbo, one of the four customs houses in China at that time. Ningbo was one of the five trading ports opened after the Opium War. In 1844, it was officially opened for foreign trade and the U.K., France, and the United States established consulates there. The Qing Government established the Customs Tax Department ("The Customs") on Zhongma Road on the north to collect taxes.

In July 1940, Japanese troops captured Zhenhai and moved to invade Ningbo. But that night the Ningbo City Defense Headquarters had assigned two Zhejiang Customs ships to transport boulders to the sea lane to stop the Japanese naval attack.

英军进攻定海

鸦片战争中，英军对浙江舟山蓄谋已久，1841年9月26日，英军三个团再犯定海。镇守定海的三位总兵葛云飞、王锡朋、郑国鸿奋起抵抗，血战六昼夜的定海保卫战是鸦片战争中敌我双方参战人数最多、规模最大、交火时间最长、伤亡最惨重的一次战役。葛云飞、王锡朋、郑国鸿三总兵同日殉国，麾下5800名守军无一变节投降。至今竹山门上，仍然到处是一座座阵亡的无名将士合葬墓。

British Troops Attacked Dinghai

British troops had long schemed to attack Zhoushan Zhejiang during the Opium War. On September 26, 1841, three British regiments attacked Dinghai, during which three commanding officers Ge Yunfei, Wang Xipeng and Deng Guohong stationed in Zhenhai led troops to fight the invaders for a difficult for six days and nights. It was the largest and longest battle with most soldiers and casualties for both sides during the Opium War. Three commanding officers died for their motherland the same day but none of their 5,800 soldiers surrendered. On Zhushan Gate there are still tombs for unknown Chinese soldiers and officers.

招宝山

招宝山在宁波市东部，明清时曾是古战场，是镇海口海防遗址的重要组成部分。登上招宝山看大海，目穷千里，波涛尽染。

Zhaobao Mountain

Located in the east of Ningbo, Zhaobao Mountain was an ancient battlefield during the Ming (1368-1644) and Qing (1644-1911) Dynasties, and is an important part of Zhenhaikou Marine Defense Ruins. From atop Zhaobao Mountain endless sea and to and fro of endless tides can be seen.

天一阁藏书阁

天一阁在宁波市老城内，是中国最早的私家藏书楼，也是世界上现存的最早三个私家藏书楼之一，建于明嘉靖年间（1522–1566）。走进天一阁，可以感受并想象古时候宁波人是如何读书、爱书和藏书的。

Tianyi Library

Located within the old Ningbo, Tianyi Library is the earliest private library in China, as well as one of the three earliest existing private libraries of the world. It was built between 1522 and 1566, during the Ming Dynasty. Visiting Tianyi Library, one can imagine how Ningbo ancestors loved, read, and collected books.

牌楼

牌楼，是有房檐的标志性、礼制性的建筑物，从汉唐宋代坊门演化而来。旧时牌楼构建主要用木、石、砖木等，多设于要道口。古时在宁波城内就有石牌坊 154 座，到处可以见到，时至今日，只剩下六七座破残骨架了，历经风雨沧桑却巍然挺立，具有极高的历史文化价值。图为原宁波老城区镇明路三门四柱石牌坊。

Archway

An archway is a symbolic and ritualistic architectural structure usually with eaves, which developed through the Han, Tang and Song Dynasties ⊠619-1127⊠. In ancient times archways were of wood, stone and/or brick built at intersecting roads. In ancient times there were 154 stone archways in Ningbo, but now, only six or seven shabby skeletons remain. However, towering erectly though suffering storms and changes, they are of very high historical, cultural value. This drawing is of the stone archway with three gates and four columns in Zhenming Road in old Ningbo.

彭山塔原貌

彭山塔在今江北区慈城镇外西南的慈江畔，是一座风水塔和航标塔，建于明代嘉靖年间（1522–1566），砖塔有 7 层，高 22 米。此塔 2005 年已重建，图为重建前原貌。

Pengshan Tower

Located on the Cijiang River bank, southwest of Cicheng Town in Jiangbei District, Pengshan Tower is a beacon tower with geomancy significance built between 1522 and 1566, during the Ming Dynasty. The 22m high brick tower with 7 floors was refurbished in 2005. The sketch depicts the tower before reconstruction.

古村小巷

宁海县前童古村，家家院前有流水、户户出门有石桥，路上铺着光溜溜的碎石板，人在巷中走，似在水中游。该村现在是国家级历史文化名村。

A Lane in the Ancient Village

In Qiantong Ancient Village of Ninghai County there is water running through every house and stone slab bridges in front of them. The lane surface is of smooth, flat paving stones.. This is a national historical and cultural village of China.

老宅

宁波的城乡老住宅门楼有点特别，构成格局严谨，轮廓肃穆庄重，很多老宅是木质结构，还采用了镂孔雕刻，做工精美，是不可多得的江南风格老住宅。

Old House

The solemn, detailed arch over the gateway of old houses in urban and rural Ningbo is quite special. Many old houses are wooden structures with carvings of exquisite workmanship typical of the rare old houses of South Yangtze River area.

村外春韵

老宁波郊外芳草碧水，诱人寻春问津，如今近山的村外依然保持古韵，良好的生态仍焕发生机无限。

Spring outside the Village

Grass and water and the mountains in the outskirts of old Ningbo attract people to admire the spring scenery and ancient appeal of the area. Here the healthy ecology helps revitalize the visitors.

航船

老宁波旧时“三江六塘河”，河道纵横，交通便捷。船是城乡频繁往返的最重要的交通工具。图为老航船过西乡望春桥的旧景。

Boats

There were “three rivers and six ponds” in old Ningbo which intersected each other, convenient for transport. Boats are the most important urban-rural transport means. The sketch is the old scene of boats passing under Wangchun Bridge in Xixiang Village.

老慈溪西门

慈溪城镇老西门有一条小河通向慈江，此图据百年前老照片绘制，当年的村镇水路是沟通古镇与外界政治、经济、文化交往的重要渠道。

Old West Gate of Cixi

There is a small river running from old West Gate in Cixi Town to the Cijiang River. The sketch is based on a century-old photo taken when the waterway was an important channel for communication with the outside world.

老宅小弄堂

小弄堂在宁波随处可见，两旁是高低错落的马头墙，中间是一条窄窄的小道，在老三区江东有“史家巷”、“打铁巷”，江北有“三宝巷”、“义庄巷”，海曙有“老实巷”、“白衣巷”等。小巷很窄、很深，深得只显出一线蓝天，望不到尽头。

Small Lane Amidst Old Houses

It is common to see small lanes everywhere in Ningbo. Like narrow paths they lie between irregular walls. There are “Shi’s Lane” and “Blacksmith Lane” in Jiangdong District; “Sanbao Lane” and “Yizhuang Lane” in Jiangbei District; and “Laoshi Lane” and “White Clothes Lane” in Haishu District. The many lanes are so narrow and deep that only a sky can be seen above.

缸鸭狗旧貌

“缸鸭狗”由江阿狗演变而成，是老宁波最有名望的汤圆店，已列入宁波市非物质文化遗产保护项目。汤圆店这百年来一直由后人继承经营。如今，老房子已毁，在宁波市万达广场仍可尝到“缸鸭狗”宁波汤圆。

Old Look of GANGYAGOU

The name of "GANGYAGOU" evolved from "JIANG'AGOU", which is the most prestigious glutinous rice ball shop in old Ningbo and listed in the Ningbo Intangible Cultural Heritage Protection Project. The shop has been managed by the same family for one hundred years; however, the old buildings have been ruined. Ningbo "GANGYAGOU" glutinous rice balls can still be enjoyed at Wanda Plaza in Ningbo.

花香后花园

老宁波民居大宅多以“院”为单元，前厅后园。后花园在宁波历史上是指有名人富户所住的房屋后面的花园，一般都种植有树木和花草，有的还有假山和鱼池。

Fragrant Back Garden

The residential houses of old Ningbo of “courtyard” style with front hall and back garden. The latter refers to gardens at the back of houses of celebrities and the rich; they generally include trees and flowers and sometimes rockeries and ponds.

冯氏贞节坊

这座据旧照片绘的是位于宁波市江北区慈城镇的“冯氏贞节坊”，高 5 米，宽 3.3 米，建于明万历年间（1573–1619）。冯有经母刘氏，在夫君死后守节不嫁，获旨兴建，今牌坊仍存，列为文保，而牌坊周边已建大量民居。

Mrs. Feng's Faithfulness Arch

It is a drawing of "Mrs. Feng's Faithfulness Arch" located in Cicheng Town, Jiangbei District, Ningbo. It is based on an old photo; it was said to be 5m tall and 3.3m wide. It was built between 1573 and 1619 during the Ming Dynasty. Liu, mother of Feng Youjing, remained faithful to her husband and did not remarry after his death. Therefore, the government built her this arch which still remains today and has been listed as a protected cultural relic. Many residential buildings have been built around the arch.

旧江夏街

“走遍天下，不如宁波江厦”是宁波人经常挂在嘴边的一句话，可见历史上的江厦街曾辉煌一时。旧时江厦街一带是商号、渔行、银楼、钱庄聚集地。灵桥、江厦桥、新江桥贯通东西南北，为宁波发展奠定了基础。

Old Jiangxia Street

Ningbo residents often say that “you can't find a better place in the world than Jiangxia in Ningbo”, which reflects the brilliant history of Jiangxia Street. Firms, fish markets, silverware shops and native banks clustered around Jiangxia Street in ancient times. Lingqiao, Jiangxia, and Xinjiang Bridges connect the streets to all directions of the city, thus laying an excellent foundation for its development.

老和丰纱厂

江东区和丰纱厂是著名的近代私人企业。和丰纱厂可溯源于 1887 年宁波北郊的通久源轧花厂，1907 年 3 月戴瑞卿、顾元琛筹资 60 万银元创办和丰纱厂。到 1936 年创纱锭总数 26000 枚的记录，和丰曾经一度成为浙江省最大的纱厂。现在，和丰部分旧址作为近代著名建筑列为文物保护单位，此图据民国期间老照片绘制。

Old Hefeng Yarn Factory

Jiangdong District Hefeng Yarn Factory is a famous modern private enterprise. Tongjiuyuan Ginning Factory, established in 1887, was the predecessor of the Hefeng Yarn Factory. In March 1903, Dai Ruiqing and Gu Yuanshen invested 600,000 taels of silver to establish Hefeng Yarn Factory. In 1936 it had a record of producing 26,000 spindles, making Hefeng Yarn Factory the largest in Zhejiang Province. Now, some old sites of Hefeng have been identified as famous modern architecture cultural relic protection sites. This sketch is drawn basing on an old photo taken during the Republic of China Period.

老当铺

在旧社会城镇当铺遍地都有。把有用的、值钱的东西当作押头兑作银子或纸币，解决家里的燃眉之急。当铺的外面或店堂里，往往写着个大得出奇的“当”字，给人一种无可奈何的感觉。此图据宁波老照片画成，当铺地点在城内药行街。

Old Pawnshop

Pawnshops could be seen everywhere in the towns of the old society. People exchanged useful or valuable things for silver or cash to relieve family financial difficulties.. An extremely large character for “Pawn” was posted outside or inside the pawnshop. This sketch is based on an old photo of Ningbo pawnshop on Yaoxing Street.

老桂花厅

桂花厅是明代建筑，位于宁波市海曙区中山广场后一条曲折的小巷中。原来的桂花厅正门上挂有一块御赐金匾，题有“孝德感天”四个字，可想当时是如何显赫。现建筑已列为文物保护。

Old Guihua Hall

Guihua Hall is a Ming Dynasty building located in a winding lane behind Zhongshan Plaza in Haishu District, Ningbo. There was a golden horizontal tablet granted by the emperor hanging in the front gate of Guahua Hall; it reads "Filial Piety Reaching Heaven". How elegant this building was at that time! Now it is a cultural relic protection unit.

古井水清

宁波古时候，没有自来水，旧时城镇乡村，用清澈的水主要还是用井水。一桶一桶从井中吊上来，滋润着人们的生活。古井水冬暖夏凉，深受人们的喜欢。图中这口古井在宁波市宁海县加爵村得巷子内，井水至今还可饮用。

Clear Ancient Well

There was no tap water in ancient Ningbo, so villagers and urban residents had to use water from wells. They fetched water from wells by the barrels for their daily use. The water in these wells is cool in summer but warm in winter and much appreciated by the people. The ancient well in this picture is located in Dexiangzi, Jiajue Village, Ninghai County, Ningbo; it still provides drinking water today.

鼓楼

鼓楼又称海曙楼，原本是唐代长庆年间明州州治衙暑子城的南门，是至今仅存的宁波古城楼遗存，是国家文物重点保护的古建筑之一，至今已有 1100 多年的历史。现在这座鼓楼是民国年间在原清代建筑物的顶上增建了消防望台和钟楼，城门进内就是公园路步行街，改名为鼓楼沿，每天人来人往，热闹非凡，成了宁波市商业文化的一个亮点。该图按 20 世纪 50 年代照片绘。

Drum Tower

Known as Haishu Tower, it was formerly the south gate of Shuzi Town, the state government office of Mingzhou during the reign of Emperor Changqing in the Tang Dynasty. It is the only surviving ancient gate tower of Ningbo and is a key relic under national protection. Over 1,100 years old, Drum Tower served as the base for the Fire Watch Platform and Bell Tower built during the Republic of China Period. There is a pedestrian walk running through the gate that has been renamed Drum Tower Street. It is very busy with people coming and going and is highlight for commercial culture in Ningbo. The sketch is drawn basing on a photo taken in the 1950s.

河姆渡

1973 年发现的 7000 多年前的河姆渡遗址，是我国目前已发现的最早的新石器时代文化遗址之一。这里出土的文物有石、玉制的装饰品，吹奏、打击乐器、骨哨、精致的象牙等。河姆渡遗址的发现，说明在长江流域同样存在着灿烂古老的新石器时代文化。

Hemudu Site

The 7,000-year old Hemudu Site discovered in 1973 is one of the earliest Neolithic cultural sites found in China. The unearthed relics from the site include stone and jade ornaments, wind and percussion musical instrument, bone whistles and exquisite ivory, etc. The discovery of this Hemudu Site proves that there was a well developed ancient Neolithic culture in the Yangtze River area.

冯宅

冯宅位于慈城镇太阳殿路 18 号，是宁波式大宅院。该宅大门向东，进深两间，有八字式封檐墙，是最美的江南古建筑之一，当代作家冯骥才老家就在这里。其中最出彩的当属冯宅中的“抱珠楼”，现在古宅已修缮。

Feng's House

Located in No. 18 Taiyangdian Road, Cicheng Town, Feng's House is a Ningbo-style mansion with east-facing gate, two rooms on each side and walls with sealed eaves. It is one of the most beautiful ancient buildings in the South Yangtze River area. It is the former home of writer Feng Jicai. The most eye-catching building is the restored "Baozhu Building".

二月放鹞子

放鹞子即放风筝。每当春天来临，宁波的田野里放鹞子的人特别多。鹞子一般用五颜六色的纸糊成，有龙、蜈蚣、鲤鱼、蝴蝶、老鹰，在春风中翩翩起舞，煞是好看。

Flying Kites in February

In Spring in the fields of Ningbo, many people fly kites, which are generally made of colorful paper in the shape of dragons, centipedes, carp, butterflies, and eagles. Kites dancing in the Spring breeze is a beautiful sight.

山乡问道

旧时宁波城里人下乡主要靠步行，特别是边远小村，只有穿过崎岖村道才能到达，一路上全靠路人指引，乡间景物令人目不暇接。

Asking Directions

In old times, city folk visited the countryside for a walk, especially to remote village; so, they had to go asking passers-by for direction along the way. The scenery is rich and interesting.

台风

台风是热带气旋的一个类别，风力往往在十二级以上，给人们的日常生活带来极大的危害，对各行各业带来不可估量的损失。宁波是沿海地区，台风带来灾害较多，所以每到台风季节，人们特别关心台风去向。

Typhoon

Typhoons are a category of tropical destructive wind power. It is extremely harmful for the daily life of the people, to agriculture and to industry. Ningbo suffers from typhoons because it is located in the coastal area; therefore, people pay great attention to the weather forecasts and the typhoon's in the typhoon season.

池塘小景

池塘是比湖泊小的水体，起到调节、储存淡水功用，因此古代宁波城乡处处可见池塘。每到夏天，池塘里蛙声阵阵；池塘中荷花盛开，池塘边的老柳树弯着腰，枝条随风舞动。旧时有的池塘里的水供人饮用，但大多数的池塘水被用作洗濯、灌田、养鱼植荷等。

The Pond

A freshwater pond is smaller than a lake. Ponds were scattered everywhere in the towns and villages of Ningbo in ancient times. Every summer frogs croaked in the ponds where lotus blossoms flourished and old willows gracefully swayed with the breeze. In old times some ponds provided drinking water for residents, but most ponds were used for washing, irrigation, fish breeding and lotus growing, etc.

永宁庵

这座江北区慈城镇西门的永宁庵，即佛教中出家的女僧修行的地方。每逢初一、十五，庵中钟鼓齐鸣、香火旺盛，善男信女们都来这里祷告，以求风调雨顺、五谷丰登。此庵今已重建，图按老照片绘制。

Yongning Temple

Yongning Temple, located at Cicheng Town's west gate, Jiangbei District, is for Buddhist nuns. Bells are rung on the first and fifteenth of the month and incense burned. Pilgrims pray for good weather and harvests. The temple has been restored ; the sketch is drawn from an old photo.

天封塔

天封塔，因建造于唐武则天天册万岁、万岁登封年间（695–696），故名“天封”，坐落在宁波大沙泥街。塔高 54.5 米，呈六角形，共 14 层，七明七暗，入地一层，曾数次遭战火灾难而重建重修。宁波古人曾把该塔视作镇邪的宝塔，现已重建，此图是百年前的旧貌。

Tianfeng Tower

Built between 695 and 696, when Empress Wu Zetian of the Tang Dynasty assumed the title of emperor, it was named "Tianfeng Tower". Located on Dashani Street, the 14-storey hexagonal tower is 54.5m tall, with seven light and seven dark storeys. There is also one storey underground. The tower has been rebuilt several times due to damage during various wars. In ancient times it was supposed to oppress evil. It has recently been restored. This sketch shows it as it appeared a hundred years ago.

天童寺

天童寺创世于晋朝，是宁波最著名的古寺之一。经唐、宋、元、明、清各个时期，历经沧桑，至今已有 1700 多年历史，寺院现存规模基本上保持明朝的格局。

Tiantong Temple

Tiantong Temple, built during the Jin Dynasty (265-420), is one of the most famous ancient temples of Ningbo; with more than 1,700 years of history, today it is basically in a Ming Dynasty (1368-1644) style.

阿育王寺

阿育王寺位于鄞州区五乡镇，始建于东晋（374 年）。因开山祖师刘萨诃结茅鄮山，闻地下有殷殷钟声，地涌舍利宝塔。据称此即古印度阿育王造八万四千塔之一，故建寺之后名为“阿育王寺”，今是我国著名古寺之一。

Asoka Temple

Located in Wuxiang Town, Yinzhou District, Asoka Temple was built in 374 during the East Jin Dynasty. It is said that ancient ancestor Liu Sahe went to Mount Mao where he heard bells ringing from an underground pagoda, one of the 84,000 pagodas of Asoka in ancient India. Thus this temple was also named “Asoka Temple” and is one of the famous ancient temples in China.

水乡路桥
Bridges in Watery Region

书院桥

位于宁波宁海县桑洲镇田洋卢村。南宋时卢氏从山东迁此耕读传家。明初卢原甲考中探花，这座单孔乱石拱桥曾是他到书院读书必经之地，故名“书院桥”。

Academy Bridge

It is located in Tianyanglu Village, Sangzhou Town, Ninghai County, Ningbo. During the Southern Song Dynasty (1127-1279), the Lu family relocated here from Shandong and earned a living from farming. During early Ming Dynasty (1368-1644), Lu Yuanjia won the honor of ranking third in imperial examination. This single-arch stone bridge connected his house and the academy; hence it was named "Academy Bridge".

骢马桥

位于江北区慈城镇即旧慈溪县县城内中心，骢马桥始建于唐开元二十六年（738 年），是古县衙门南街河上石桥，此桥在明代重建，是城内最高大单孔石拱桥，桥边即船埠。

Horse Bridge

Located in downtown Cixi, today's Cicheng Town, Jiangbei District, Horse Bridge, built in 738, during the Tang Dynasty, was built over the Nanjie River near the yamen. Rebuilt during the Ming Dynasty (1368-1644), the bridge was the largest single-arch stone bridge in town. There was a dock next to the bridge.

黄公桥

位于宁海县黄坛镇杨家村，单孔石拱建于清代，桥在宁波至台州的古驿道上，据称汉代黄石公在此留有遗迹，故名“黄公”。明代大旅行家徐霞客曾过此桥去天台山。

Huanggong Bridge

Located in Yangjia Village, Huangtan Town, Ninghai County, this single-arch stone bridge was built during the Qing Dynasty (1644-1911) along the ancient road from Ningbo to Taizhou. Legend has it that in the Han Dynasty (206 BC – 220 AD) Huang Shi left a relic here. Xu Xiake, a famous traveler of the Ming Dynasty (1368-1644), traveled to Tiantai Mountain via this bridge.

鲒溪桥

位于鄞州区五乡镇东塘河上，因桥跨大河，在清代重建三孔石拱桥，长达 30 米，势如卧龙，故又称“鄞东第一桥”。

Jiaoxi Bridge

Spanning the big Dongtang River in Wuxiang Town, Yinzhou District, this bridge was rebuilt with three arches during the Qing Dynasty (1644-1911). It is 30m long and resembles a reclining dragon; it is known as "The Largest Bridge in Yindong".

宏济桥

位于宁海县前童镇庙山村，单孔块石拱，建于嘉庆十七年（1812年），采用石料肋拱构造，故桥体镂空，十分科学，桥虽不大，但是很精巧，过桥即有一座古庙、两棵古柏。

Hongji Bridge

Located in Miaoshan Village, Qiantong Town, Ninghai County, the single-arch stone bridge was built in 1812, during the Qing Dynasty. Made of aggregate rock, the bridge said to be hollow, is somewhat of a scientific, special structure. At one end of the delicate bridge stand an ancient temple and two ancient cypresses.

白云桥

位于余姚鹿亭乡的中村，四面环山，与青山白云为伴。桥始建于唐代，重建于清代，由于石拱桥以山岩、溪石为基，故避开了洪水冲突，如今桥体完好。

White Cloud Bridge

Located in Zhongcun Village of Yuyao Luting Town, Ningbo, the bridge is said to be "embraced by mountains and accompanied by clouds. It was built during the Tang Dynasty (618-907) and rebuilt during the Qing Dynasty (1644-1911). It h as avoided destruction from floods because of the abutments of boulders which surround it.

白岩桥

位于余姚与鄞州区接界的深山溪谷中，三孔，乱石起拱，以山岩桥基桥墩，桥靠近余姚市陆埠镇大坪地村，民国时重建，是古时这一地区的重要交通要道。

White Rock Bridge

Spanning a mountain brook at the border of Yuyao and Yinzhou Districts, this three-arch stone bridge is protected by rock abutments. Adjacent to Dapingdi Village, Lubu Town, Yuyao, it was rebuilt during the Republic of China Period (1912-1949). It lay on an important transportation route in ancient times.

福泉桥

位于余姚河姆渡村，桥始建于明代，长 17 米，光绪七年（1881 年）重建，是余姚市通向宁波市姚江南岸古道的必经之路。由于桥建在福泉山下，故称福泉桥。

Fuquan Bridge

Located in Hemudu Village, Yuyao, this 17 meter-long bridge was built during the Ming Dynasty (1368-1644) and rebuilt in 1881. It is the key passage way from Yuyao to the south bank of the Yaojiang River in Ningbo. Built at the foot of Fuquan Mountain, it is called Fuquan Bridge.

永济桥

又称长山桥，坐落于北仑区小港镇长山村小峡江上，始建于宋代，明清时重建重修，是当地近海最大的一座石桥。

Yongji Bridge

Known as Changshan Bridge, it is located over Xiaoxia River in Changshan Village, Xiaogang Town, Beilun District Built during the Song Dynasty (960-1279) and rebuilt in the Ming and Qing Dynasties it is the largest stone bridge in the area.

夹田桥

位于江北区慈城镇南门，是一座高大的石拱桥，据说当年住在桥两边的农民为分田地而闹矛盾打官司，县太爷分好地后，两户人家中间隔一大河，造一桥为界，故称夹田桥。此桥已重建为水泥桥，此图按老照片绘。

Jiatian Bridge

This high, stone arch bridge is located at the south gate of Cicheng Town, Jiangbei District. It is said that farmers on two sides of the bridge had a dispute over the nearby fields and sued in the Yamen. The county magistrate delineated the field borders and the farmers built this bridge to mark the border, therefore it was called Jiatian Bridge. It was later rebuilt with concrete; the sketch is based on an old photo.

二眼碶桥

位于象山县晓塘乡后岭村。九龙江的入海口，建了一座既可蓄水的碶闸又可通行往来的石板桥。桥与碶虽都不起眼，但功能充分发挥。

Eryan Bridge

Located in Houling Village, Xiaotang Town, Xiangshan County, the bridge was built over the estuary of Nine-Dragon River and serves as passage for foot traffic. Although it is not a famous bridge, it has long played an important functions.

惠明桥

桥名有“惠泽明州”之意。双孔石拱桥始建于唐代，是千年之前古明州州治鄞西小溪镇交通要津。碑记说此桥“溉禾稼、通舟楫，农作旅行赖以为安。”

Huimin Bridge

Meaning "Benefiting the Mingzhou", this double-arch stone bridge was built during the Tang Dynasty (618-907) and has long served as an important passage for Xiaoxi Town, Yinxi, Mingzhou. The monument says this bridge " lets vessels through and makes travelers safe."

太平桥

这是据 1865 年英国旅行家所摄旧照所绘的位于慈溪南门城外三座桥中的一座太平桥，现已改建为水泥桥。

Taiping Bridge

This is Taiping Bridge, one of three bridges outside the South Gate in Cixi, as sketched from an old photo taken by a British traveler in 1865. Now it has been rebuilt as a concrete bridge.

朱家渡桥

位于市北仑区小港镇朱家渡村。此地小峡江江阔水深，原来仅靠渡船往返于两岸。明代万历三十二年（1604 年），村中善士出资建桥，五孔石梁，俗称“五眼桥”。

Zhujiadu Bridge

It is located in Zhujiadu Village, Xiaogang Town, Beilun District. Xiaoxia River is wide and deep. In the past, people had to take a ferry to cross the river but In 1604, a wealthy man of the village funded the bridge with five arches; thus, it is commonly known as “five arches bridge”.

达蓬桥

位于慈溪市三北镇达蓬山。因村南有一座达蓬山，记载秦始皇派徐福从此地东渡蓬莱，故村中一座不大的石梁桥名曰“达蓬”，建于清代。

Dapeng Bridge

Built during the Qing Dynasty (1644-1911), the bridge is located near Dapeng Mountain, Sanbei Town, Cixi. Dapeng Mountain is south of the village. It was across that mountain. Emperor Qin Shihhuang of the Qin Dynasty (221-206 BC) sent Xu Fu to visit Penglai in the east; this small stone bridge is called “Dapeng Bridge”.

天戏亭桥

位于丘隘镇横泾村，建于清代嘉庆年间，桥面宽达三米，与风雨亭连起来有 5 米，因此桥上可演戏，桥头两岸和船上都是看戏场。戏亭桥是水乡特有的风景。

Drama Pavilion Bridge

Located in Hengjing Village, Qiu'ai Town, the 3m wide bridge was built during the reign of Qing Emperor Jiajing (1796-1820) just 5 meters from Rain-Shield Pavilion. Performance can be staged on the bridge and people can watch from both banks or from boats. Drama Pavilion Bridge is the unique site.

尚源桥

桥建于清代，位于宁海县深甽镇大蔡村的凫溪之源，是一座小型的单孔五开间木梁屋盖式廊桥。

Shangyuan Bridge

This small, single-arch wood roofed bridge was built during the Qing Dynasty (1644-1911) at the source of Fuxi Brook in Dacai Village, Shenzhen Town, Ninghai County.

东岗碶桥

位于北仑区小港镇东岗碶村，既是一座蓄泻江水的碶闸，又是一座沟通二岸的石桥。村边有东岗山，碶闸桥石砌十三孔，建于明代万历三十一年（1603 年）。

Donggangqi Bridge

Located in Donggangqi Village, Xiaogang Town, Beilun District, the bridge also serves as a floodgate to store water. Donggang Mountain from which the bridge gets its name lies near the village. This bridge with its 13 arches was built in 1603 during the Ming Dynasty.

迎春桥

位于宁海县岔路镇大水路村，此处海拔 500 米，在 1948 年，当地村民采用石板直拱三折边建造了跨溪石桥，因地制宜解决了出行不便的问题。

Yingchun Bridge

Located in Dashuilu Village, Chalu Town, Ninghai County, the bridge is 500m above sea level. In 1948, local residents built this bridge with flat-arch and three-stone slab construction over the brook to facilitate the traffic.

双邑桥

位于余姚牟山镇与绍兴市小曹娥镇相隔于一河，故名“双邑”。桥建于清代道光十五年（1835 年），三孔石梁，桥畔有市集。

Double-town Bridge

Located between Moushan Town, Yuyao, and Xiaocao'er Town of Shaoxing, it earns the name "Double-Town Bridge". The three-arch stone bridge was built in 1835 during the Qing Dynasty. There is a marketplace next to the bridge.

会龙桥

又称李家塔板桥，位于余姚鹿亭乡，桥为二孔，木梁直柱墩，盖有桥屋。故桥下有利山洪排泄，桥上可供交通和歇息遮蔽风雨，桥又在两水交会处，故又名“会龙桥”。

Huilong Bridge

Known as Li's Plate Bridge, it is a two-arch, wooden abutment bridge located in Luting Town, Yuyao. This covered bridge provides shelter for passers-by on rainy days and a place for tired travelers to rest. The bridge spans the confluence of two rivers, so it is called "Huilong Bridge".

泮池桥

位于江北区慈城镇内，“泮”是中国文字中专用于孔庙学官的专用字，因此，旧时孔庙又称“泮宫”，庙内石桥一般三孔，又称泮桥。这座泮池桥始建于宋代，明清时期重修。

Panchi Bridge

This bridge is located in Cicheng Town, Jiangbei District. “Pan” is a Chinese character to describe instructors of Confucius temples; therefore, Confucian temples were known as “Pan Palaces” in the old times. Stone bridges in temples usually have three arches, so they are called Pan Bridges. Panchi Bridge was built during the Song Dynasty (960-1279) and reconstructed during the Ming and Qing Dynasties.

五龙桥

位于鄞州区姜山镇五龙村，此村因有五条河港交汇于村外而名。桥始建清代道光五年（1825年）。三孔石梁，桥上刻有五条龙，故名“五龙桥”。

Five-Dragon (Wu Long) Bridge

Located in Wulong Village, Jiangshan Town, Yinzhou District, it was built in 1825, during the Qing Dynasty. Wulong Village got the name from five nearby intersecting rivers. The three-arch stone bridge has five dragons engraved on it, so it is called "Five-Dragon Bridge".

运河桥

　　位于慈溪市鸣鹤村的街河上，桥建于明代，清咸丰九年（1859 年）重修，条石砌筑单孔的石拱桥曾是街河上集市中心地。

Canal Bridge

Located over the river in Minghe Village, Cixi, the bridge was built during the Ming Dynasty (1368-1644) and reconstructed in 1859 during the Qing Dynasty. The single-arch stone bridge was built with stone plates that used to be the central marketplace.

四明山镇东桥

位于四明山镇高山上。桥为一孔石砌廊桥，建于明代，为村民出行提供了方便，桥下溪水可流向山外。

Simingshan Town East Bridge

Located in the mountains of Simingshan Town, this single-arch stone bridge was built during the Ming Dynasty (1368-1644) for the convenience for villagers.

光溪桥

位于鄞州区鄞江镇，因鄞江镇古称光溪镇，桥以镇名，始建于明代，清代重修，这是一座建造十分规整的石拱桥，保存也很完好。

Guangxi Bridge

This bridge is located in Yinjiang Town Yinzhou District, which was known as Guangxi Town in ancient times; so, the bridge takes the name of the town. This well preserved stone bridge built during the Ming Dynasty (1368-1644) and reconstructed during the Qing Dynasty (1644-1911).

西门廊桥

位于江北区慈城镇西门，江南因雨水较多，桥上有一房子似走廊，借以避雨，故以廊桥为名，现已荡然无存。

West Gate Lounge Bridge

Located at the west gate of Cicheng Town, Jiangbei District, this covered bridge provided a room or lounge-like space very convenient for the rainy season in the South of the Yangtze area,thus getting the name Lounge Bridge. Unfortunately this bridge no longer exists.

彩虹桥

位于老慈溪县城慈湖中，石拱桥，桥洞高圆，象似彩虹而名，一直流传至今。

Rainbow Bridge

Located in Cihu Lake in old Cixi Town, this stone bridge has a high, round arch resembling a rainbow, thus getting the name.

五乡碶桥

位于鄞州五乡镇，此处河港宽阔，河水经桥下通向江海。桥始建于宋代，清代重建，三联石拱，沟通附近五个乡镇交通往来。

Wuxiang Bridge

Located in Wuxiang Town, Yinzhou where the rivers flowing to the sea are wide, this bridge was built during the Song Dynasty (960-1279) and restored during the Qing Dynasty (1644-1911). The three-arch stone bridge connect five villages and towns nearby.

万安桥

位于余姚梨洲街道金冠村，桥建于清代，采用三折边单孔直拱，结构科学，适应山区就地取材，沟通往来。

Wan’an Bridge

Located in Jinguan Village, Lizhou Sub-District, Yuyao, the bridge was built during the Qing Dynasty (1644-1911), following the scientific “three folded edges and single flat arch” structure. It fits the local geographical conditions and is convenience for traffic.

通济桥

位于余姚市城内的余姚江上，始建于宋代，元代至顺三年（1332 年）改建为三孔块石拱桥，名曰“通济”，取《诗经》中“舟楫之利，以济不通”之意。

Tongji Bridge

Spanning the Yuyao River within Yuyao, it was built during the Song Dynasty (960-1279) and expanded to a three-arch stone bridge in 1332 during the Yuan Dynasty. The name “Tongji” refers to “connecting places by boat” in “Book of Songs”.

月湖桥

位于宁波市城内月湖中心的单孔石拱桥，因湖形如月，故名“月湖”。桥始建于宋代，明清时期重修。

Moon-Lake Bridge

This single-arch stone bridge located on Moon Lake in downtown Ningbo got its name because it resembles a moon. The bridge was built during the Song Dynasty (960-1279) and reconstructed in the Ming and Qing Dynasties.

长安廊桥

位于奉化溪口镇栖霞坑村，是一座单孔石拱风雨廊桥，建于清代。廊桥成为古村南北交通要道，又是村民歇息之处。

Chang'an Lounge Bridge

Located in Xixiakeng Village, Xikou Town, Fenghua, this single-arch covered bridge built during the Qing Dynasty (1644-1911) was an important route connecting south to north in the ancient village, as well as a place for villagers to take a rest.

郭塘桥

位于江北区慈城镇西郊，因桥架在郭塘岙流来郭塘河而名桥。桥造于宋代，明代重修，为三孔二排柱斜插石墩，长 12 米，上铺五块石板，造型古朴，结构稳固。

Guotang Bridge

Located in west suburb of Cicheng Town, Jiangbei District, this bridge was named after the Guotang River. Built during the Song Dynasty (960-1279) and reconstructed in the Ming Dynasty, this stone bridge with two rows of pillars is 12 meters long. Each span has five simple but sturdy stone plates.

灵桥

位于奉化江上，始建于唐代，原来是用十六舟联结的浮桥，后建桥时空中现彩虹，故名“灵现”，简称灵桥。1936 年在宁波同乡会资助下由德国西门子公司承建，重建成钢梁混凝土缓拱桥。

Bridge of Hope

Spanning Fenghua River, a floating bridge was built here during the Tang Dynasty (618-907) with 16 boats. When the bridge was completed, a rainbow appeared overhead; the people regarded this as a good omen and called it "Bridge of Hope". In 1936, it was rebuilt as concrete steel beam bridge, by Siemens Corporation with funds from the Ningbo Township Association.

老新江桥

位于宁波市的三江口，因建此桥前江上已有“老江桥”，故此桥名“新江桥”，用 18 艘木船上铺板成桥，建于 1842 年。1990 年改建为五跨四墩钢筋混凝土大桥。

Old Xinjiang Bridge

Located in Sanjiangkou of Ningbo, there was already a Laojiang (Old River) Bridge here before “Xinjiang (New River) Bridge”, made from 18 wooden boats was built in 1842 as seen in this sketch. It was rebuilt in 1990 as a five-span reinforced concrete bridge.

行当习俗

辞旧迎新

老宁波人每逢旧历过年前一周要在居宅内外清洗打扫。这是迎接新年的重要环节，表达了对新年的除旧迎新思想，使家家户户干干净净、欢欢喜喜过新年。不仅长辈忙碌，孩子们也参与其中。

Cleaning for the New Year

Old Ningbo citizens cleaned the entire house a week before Chinese New Year, as a traditional Chinese way to welcome in the New Year with everything all clean and fresh. Children as well as the elders were busy with this effort.

跑马灯

跑马灯在宁波也叫走马灯。原用毛竹编织成马头、马尾，糊上颜色鲜艳的纸，如今彩纸已由丝绸代替，表演时系在身上。一般在春节等喜庆的日子里与大头娃娃一起到街头巷尾去演出，是老宁波喜闻乐见的民间艺术。

Flow Lamp

Originally lamps of woven bamboo were made into horse bodies, on which colorful paper was pasted. Later the paper was replaced by silk making it easier for performers to wear them on their bodies. Generally people wear these silk horse bodies and big doll heads to show off along streets for New Year and other celebrations; these costumes are popular folk art of Ningbo.

腊八粥

腊八粥原是每年农历腊月初八日佛陀成道纪念日这天佛教寺庵施给民众的“腊八粥”。腊八粥用多种食材熬制而成：大米、糯米、莲子、花生、赤豆、红枣、冰糖等，也叫七宝五味粥。后来腊八粥的习俗已非佛门所有，而成为一种民间习俗流传至今。

Laba Porridge

Originally a kind of porridge that Buddhist temples gave the public on the memorial day when the Buddha reached enlightenment, December 8 on the lunar calendar, Laba Porridge is cooked with a variety of ingredients, i.e., rice, glutinous rice, lotus seeds, peanuts, beans, red dates, crystal sugar. It is also known as Seven-Ingredient Porridge. Later, having Laba Porridge became a wide-spread folk custom that has been passed down to modern times.

清明上坟

清明是我国农历二十四节气之一，是我国传统节日，也是重要的祭祀节日，“清明时节雨纷纷，路上行人欲断魂”，清明祭祖和扫墓是我国民间的一种重要风俗，最早始于汉代，一直延续到今天。古时的宁波人常常把一串串纸钱挂在坟头上，然后烧香祭祖，以示怀念。

Tomb-Sweeping at Qingming Festival

Qingming is one of 24 solar terms of China tradition, as well as the traditional and important ritual festival. "Drizzle never stop around Qingming Festival, making people so sad about the death of passed loved ones." It is an important folk custom for Chinese to worship ancestors and tidy their tombs during Qingming Festival; a practice which started during the Han Dynasty (206 BC-220 AD). In ancient times, Ningbo folk would hang strings of paper money on the grave mound and burn incense to worship their ancestors.

端午节

农历五月初五是传统的端午节，始于春秋战国时期，至今已有 2000 多年的历史。端午也是宁波十分盛行的隆重节日，家家户户挂艾叶、菖蒲辟邪，做香袋，吃粽子，中午喝一口雄黄酒意除百病百毒。

Dragon Boat Festival

May 5 of lunar calendar is the traditional Dragon Boat Festival, which started from the Spring and Autumn Period (722-481 BC), over 2,000 years ago. It is a very grand festival in Ningbo, in which every household hangs mugwort and calamus to drive away evil. In addition, they would make sachets, eat rice dumplings and sip Realgar wine at noon to drive away illness and toxins.

中秋月夜

“明月几时有？把酒问青天。”这是苏轼在中秋节晚上的对月抒怀。通过想象设问，展现中秋月亮的奇景，中秋月夜最美好，宁波人往往把中秋节定在八月十六，据史料记载，当时宁波籍南宋丞相史浩母亲生日为八月十六，将中秋节退后一天，日久成俗。该天一家人一起观赏月色，品尝月饼，共享天伦之乐。

Mid-Autumn Night

“When can I have my full moon? I raise my wine bottle to the heaven, asking.” This is a poem by Su Shi, the great poet of the Northern Song Dynasty (960-1127), written on night of Mid-Autumn Day. He described the wonderful scene of the moon on Mid-Autumn Day through imagination and questioning. The night at Mid-Autumn Day is the most beautiful, but Ningbo citizens always have Mid-Autumn Day on August 16 of lunar calendar. The historical records indicate that the birthday of the mother of Shi Hao, Prime Minister of the Southern Song Dynasty who was native Ningbo, was August 16 in lunar calendar; so, they made it a custom to celebrate the Mid-Autumn Day a day later. The family would watch the moon and eat moon cakes together that day to enjoy the reunion.

办满月酒

旧时宁波人长辈为了庆祝宝宝来到这个世界上满一个月而举办的邀请亲友共同参与的宴会，称为满月酒。宁波人爱面子，往往把满月酒办得很丰盛，亲朋好友也会客气地送上红包表示祝贺。.

One-month Celebration

In Ningbo in the old days the elders would organize a feast to celebrate the first month of the newly born baby. They would invite friends and relatives to the party, which is called one-month celebration. Being sensitive to their reputation, Ningbo people would have an extremely grand celebration while friends and relatives would present money in red envelopes for congratulation.

堕米嫂

堕米嫂是生活在社会底层的出家人，但不生活在尼姑庵里。堕米嫂从事的职业，往往是给出嫁的新娘化妆，诸如修眉毛、绞脸上的汗毛等。

Bride-Caring Sister-in-law

Bride-caring sister-in-law refers to a nun living at the bottom of society but not living in a nunnery. Bride-caring sister-in-law would earn money by helping brides to put on make-up, beautifying the eyebrows and removing hairs on the face.

乡间古韵

老宁波民居凡高墙护卫，马头墙高耸必为名门望族居处。岁月流逝、几经风雨，留存至今的已不多了。

Ancient Charm in the Countryside

Old Ningbo residential houses have tall walls for security reasons. Towering walls indicate the house for celebrities and the wealthy. However, few such houses remain in Ningbo due to social conditions through time.

黄花闺女

人们常常把未婚的姑娘称为黄花闺女，因为古时未婚女子在梳妆打扮时喜欢在脸上贴素雅的黄花，这样既能引起人们的注意，又能说明自己的身份。

Virgin

People often call unmarried girls virgins. In ancient times, unmarried girls would put simple yet elegant yellow flower in their hair to attract attention and indicate their available status.

书香门第

这种老墙门住的是“书香子弟”，祖祖辈辈大都是读书人。他们在乡镇中都颇有威望，不仅识字明理，还较为富有，门内外院子也干净宽敞。

Home for Scholars

Usually scholars lived in houses with old walls. Their senior generations were scholars too. Since they were learned and sensible with considerable wealth, they enjoyed high prestige in the town and lived in clean, spacious courtyard house.

卖膏药

每逢集市，在宁波街头巷尾常常有卖拳头、做大力士的表演，节目多为卧钉板、敲石板等惊险动作，最后是推销祖传的伤膏伤药，看的人有男女老幼，各行各业的人。

Selling Ointment Sticking-plaster

There always Kung Fu and “strong man” shows on the streets in Ningbo during market fairs. The performers would lie on nail beds with a piece of heavy slate on their bellies; the slate would then be punched and broken, but the purpose of the performance was to sell ointment sticking-plaster. Often, they would attract audiences from all walks of life -- old and young, men and women.

剃头匠

昔日称剃头匠，现在称理发师，昔日宁波城乡很多挑着理发工具的剃头匠，这些工匠手艺精湛，挑着担子，走街串巷，热情为老百姓服务，并以此为生。

Barber

Known as barbers in the past, they are called hair-stylists today. In old days there were many barbers carrying their tools through towns and villages in Ningbo to serve the folk and make a living. They all were skilled at their work.

补碗补缸

补缸补碗是古时三百六十行之一，多是江西人在宁波走街串户，为各家各户有裂缝的瓷碗缸甏等进行修复，以延长使用时间，并节省日常开支。

Fixing Bowls and Pots

This was one of the 360 industries in ancient times -- fixing bowl and pots. People, mostly from Jiangxi, would repair cracked ceramic bowls and vats for Ningbo households to extend the life of ceramic ware and save replacement costs.

箍桶匠

旧时宁波人有女儿出嫁要备各种嫁妆，这样就要请箍桶匠来做提桶、脚桶、马桶、果桶等。箍桶匠用箍将做桶的木板捆在一起，迫使其成为所需要的形状，确保接缝严实。在 20 世纪 80 年代前还经常看到，挑着一副担子，嘴里不断吆喝着“箍桶噢！箍桶噢！”的箍桶匠，走村串巷为老百姓制作、修理各种木桶制品。

Barrel Maker

In old days, Ningbo families would hire barrel makers to make barrels for water, foot-washing, toilets and fruit when they had daughter to be married. Barrel makers bound all the wooden slats together tightly. There were barrel makers as late as the 1980s who carried a pair of bamboo baskets and yelled “Barrel making, barrel making” through streets and made and repaired wooden barrels for the folk.

磨剪刀

过去，在宁波的街头巷尾，常常会听到“磨剪刀来，抢菜刀！”的吆喝声。生活中剪刀、菜刀常用会变钝，需要磨薄，于是就产生了磨剪刀这一行当。在宁波这一行当往往以江西老年男人为主，有的已定居在宁波。

Grinding Scissors

In the past, the call of "grinding knife, grinding scissors" could be heard on the streets. Scissors and knives always dull with use so need frequent grinding, which gave birth to this service. Usually old men from Jiangxi provided service in Ningbo; some later settled in Ningbo.

咸光饼

咸光饼是宁波土特产，一种干巴巴的小面饼，外表光溜溜的，像小孩的光头，吃起来咸滋滋，香喷喷的，这普普通通的面饼，相传是几百年前抗倭名将戚继光为抵抗倭寇，防止将士饥饿，把一串串咸味的小圆饼挂在胸前，后来演变成咸光饼也是宁波人对抗倭先贤的纪念。

Salty Cake

This is a native product of Ningbo - a kind of dry bread that has a smooth surface like the bare head of child, but it is fragrant and tastes salty. Legend has it that several hundred years ago anti-Japanese hero Jiang Jiguang made salty round cakes to hang on the neck of soldiers so they would not get hungry during battle. Later, this common salty cake became a memorial for Ningbo people to memorialize anti-Japanese heroes.

卜课算命

旧时候卜课算命的人称为算命先生，这种职业在宁波往往以男性为主，有一些生活无着的盲人，或初通“周易”知识，进行卜课算命排“八字”。旧时战事不断，民不聊生，老百姓生活饥寒交迫，算命便成为人们唯一的精神寄托。

Fortune Telling

Fortune-telling was a common career in the old days. Men in Ningbo would take this career. Some were blind and, once they had studied the Book of Changes, they would tell the fate for people according to their birthday". In past years life was difficult for people, so fortune telling became the only spiritual sustenance for them.

爆米花

每当春节来临，老宁波家家户户都准备新年吃食，其中米花、年糕家家必备。因为做年糕能获得一个好彩头："年糕年糕年年高，一年更比一年好！"有的人家还把年糕切片晾干，或将糯米准备好，等待有做爆米花生意的，在老宅门口用炉火做爆米花和年糕干。

Popcorn

Old Ningbo households would prepare food for the Spring Festival to include popcorn and rice cake. Rice cake implies good luck - life will be better than ever! Some families would cut rice cake into pieces and dry them, or they would prepare glutinous rice to make popcorn and dry rice cake on the stove outside the door when the popcorn maker went by.

大院小明堂

老宁波的古宅屋角高跷，内立花墙，建有厅堂。厅堂前得一块露天场地称为“明堂”。旧时主人必定经常打扫，布置古雅整洁。

Open “Hall” in Courtyard

Ancient houses of old Ningbo have high roofs, screen walls and halls. There is an open area in front of the hall known as “open hall” or courtyard. The owner of the house would clean it often and decorate it with elegantly and quaintly.

牌楼训女

旧宁波有为孤妇烈女立牌楼之俗。进入近代社会后，封建礼教解体，然而偶有女子犯了“礼法”，族中人就在牌坊前训教女儿。

Teaching Daughter in Archway

In old Ningbo virtuous widows and heroic women would have archways erected in their honor to praise their noble behavior. However, in modern times, some women may offend the current "etiquette"; in such cases, the family will lecture their daughter in front of the archway.

过桥赶集

集市日是宁波人民间商贸交易活动。旧时为了方便进行商品交易，人们就确定一个时间作为集市日，或十日一市、十日三市。其实是一个综合性的物资交易的日子。集市日那天，街上商品琳琅满目，五花八门。赶集的人摩肩接踵，热闹非凡。此图为鄞西林村过万安桥赶市日。

Market Fair Over the Bridge

Ningbo folks have Market Fairs. In order to facilitate commodity transaction in the old days, people set a fixed day for a market fair, namely, one every ten days or three market fairs in ten days. Actually they were days for general commodity transactions when specific commodities would be on sale.

There were crowds of people in the market fair, making an extremely busy scene. This sketch shows the Wan'an Bridge Market Fair in Yinxilin Village.

牌楼路口

明清的牌楼多为石制，既有礼制纪念性内容，又有地标性作用，这座石牌坊原来立在宁波城内南门入口，现仅存残柱。

Archway Intersection

Archways in the Ming and Qing Dynasties were mostly made of stone, and had l commemoration significance and served as important landmarks. This stone archway was originally erected at south gate within Ningbo. Now it only has a few remaining pillars.

念佛婆婆

江南农村很多人信仰佛教，念佛婆婆在宁波曾风行一时，相信佛教的婆婆们，天天吃素念经，早晚烧香拜佛，以求家庭平安，健康长寿，多子多福，财源滚滚。

Buddhism Practicing Grandma

Many villagers in the South of Yangtze River believe in Buddhism, so grandmas practicing Buddhism were common in Ningbo. They ate vegetables and chanted every day; they burnt incense to worship the Buddha and pray for peace, health, longevity, descendants and wealth.

办学堂

有些村庄孩子们没有读书的地方，娃娃们上学都要到很远的城里去读书，于是一些有经济实力和文化头脑的人就在附近创办了学堂，让孩子们就近读书，这是一种公益事业，深受老百姓的欢迎。

Schools

There were no schools in some villages; so, children had to walk to the school in towns far away. Therefore, some wealthy, cultivated people built schools nearby to provide schooling for local children -- public welfare welcomed by villagers.

小学堂

旧时农村小学堂是把过去聚集在一个小村的儿童组织起来，到附近的一个宅院读书识字，教书先生往往也是在当地聘请，教训古文有《三字经》、《山海经》、《唐诗》《宋词》等。

Primary School

"Three Character Primer", *"Classic of Mountains and Rivers"*, *"Poems of the Tang Dynasty"* and *"Poem Lyrics of the Song Dynasty"*, etc.

私塾女教师

宁波旧时，乡镇办起了小学，首先要学写字、认字。写字一般用毛笔，是书法中难度最大的。私塾中女教师在教入学孩童练些毛笔字。

Female Teacher in Private School

Towns in Ningbo had primary schools in old days to help pupils practice writing and reading. Usually, they practiced with a calligraphy brush which is difficult to use well.Female teachers in private schools taught children brush writing.

女学生聚会

宁波在百余年前就办了“女学”。有许多知识女性，逃离封建家庭，进入女学堂读书或终身以教书为生，这图画的是一群旧时女学生聚会情景。

Gathering of Girl Students

Ningbo allowed girls to go to school one hundred years ago. Many educated girls fled from their feudal family to study or teach in female school. This sketch shows a group of girl students gathering in old days.

问路

旧时农村没有地名记号，找人必须问当地人，往往费尽周折。

Asking Directions

In old days there weren't any names for roads in villages; so, people had to ask the way. It was usually a painstaking process.

收旧货业

古时候，大户人家往往把多余的旧器物、红木家具卖给收旧货的人。收旧货的人挑着担子或者拉着车子，走街串巷，现时仍有收旧货的职业，只是少有走街串巷而已。图为在城内街巷中收购旧货的老人。

Rag-and-Bone Merchant

In ancient times, a wealthy family would sell excess old artifacts and mahogany furniture to “rag-and-bone” merchants who would carry bamboo basket or pushcarts through the streets to collect second-hand goods. There are still rag-and-bone merchants, but they seldom wander about the streets. This sketch shows an old rag-and-bone merchant on the lane.

老信客

清代晚期，宁波较大的城镇已通邮。古时的宁波人称邮递员为老信客。是一种非常辛苦的职业，默默无闻地为生活奔波，但一般在社会上信誉较好，老信客能突出一个“信”字，与千家万户送信，一丝不苟。

Old Messenger

In the late Qing Dynasty (1644-1911) there was mail service in larger towns in Ningbo. In ancient times a postman was known as an old messenger in Ningbo. It was a very difficult job. Old messengers strove quietly for a living; but, they enjoyed a good reputation in society, because they meticulously delivered letters to thousands of families.

别家谋业

宁波人称学徒为“学生意”，顾名思义，就是去商店或者工厂学习技术和谋生的本领。学徒工作生活很辛苦，待遇很低，有的甚至光吃口饭没有工资，学徒期往往为三年，期满后才能正式开始工作。很多宁波家庭将子女送到外埠学生意。

Career in Another's House

Ningbo people called apprenticeships "learning business", which means the inexperienced learning skills to make a living in a shop or factory. It was a tough life for apprentices, because they only got meager pay. Some only got meals in three years of apprenticeship without any payment. They started to work officially after the apprenticeship. Many Ningbo residents sent their children to learn business abroad.

红帮裁缝

原是清代晚期至民国期间流行在宁波东乡的民间手工艺。红帮裁缝的精湛西服制作工艺如今是宁波的一项非物质文化遗产。老宁波人称西洋人为“红毛”，所以“红帮裁缝”意思是为西洋人做的服装。红帮裁缝制作的西装、旗袍、中山装讲究高要求的合身、美观。红帮裁缝至今传承不衰。

Hongbang Tailor

It was originally a folk craft of Dongxiang Ningbo during late Qing Dynasty (1644-1911) and the Republic of China. The superb suit making craftsmanship of Hongbang tailors has become an intangible cultural heritage of Ningbo. Old Ningbo folk called foreigners “red hair”, so Hongbang tailor refers to making suits for Westerners. Business suits, cheongsam, and Chinese tunic suits made by Hongbang tailors emphasize fit and appearance; so, the craftsmanship has been carefully passed down.

木厂锯木匠

甬江边有木行路，经营南北木材，大木需用拉锯锯开，门口兼作工场。

Wood Factory Carpenter

This is a wood factory by the bank of the Yongjiang River, which uses timbers from south and north China. Large timbers need to be cut by saws. The sketch depicts life in front of the a workshop.

打铁作坊

老宁波俗语“天下三样苦：打铁、撑船、磨豆腐。”宁波慈城莫家巷在 20 世纪 80 年代还可以看到传统的打铁作坊，两位铁匠钳住火红铁块，相向轮流捶打。

Blacksmith Workshop

There is an old saying in Ningbo: "There are three tough jobs - blacksmith, boating and making tofu." In Mojia Lane in Cicheng Ningbo, there was traditional blacksmith workshop in the 1980s. Two blacksmiths held the red iron with tongs and pounded on it in turn.

老宅鞋匠

在近代宁波城乡流行布鞋，鞋底由鞋匠家庭女性叠碎布用鞋底针连麻棉的纱搓成的粗线，密集穿钉而成，宁波人叫“砌鞋底”。鞋面按图样用零头布剪成。鞋底、鞋面交鞋匠手工缝连，撑开，就是鞝鞋了。鞋匠多流动于城乡，买鞋、修制、定制都可。图中修鞋摊摆在宁波邮政局对面的鞋匠，此图据老照片绘制。

Shoemaker in Old House

Cloth shoes were popular in urban and rural areas in Ningbo in modern times. The soles are made by cloth waste and yarn threads twisted by housewives. The threads are densely sewn on the cloth waste, so local people call them “assembled soles”. Vamps are made with pieces of cloth according to a pattern, and then the shoemakers sews the soles with vamps, which is completed whenthe vamp is braced up from the sole. Shoemakers traveled to towns and villages to sell, repair and custom-make shoes. The sketch, which is drawn according to an old photo, shows the shoe-repair stall opposite Ningbo Post Office.

圆木箍桶

走街的箍桶匠挑着工具担，沙哑的吆喝声在小巷回荡“打圈哈！打－圈－哈－！”这是给各家修理木制的盆桶、高镂盖的。家用的木制品，时日久了就会散，必须重新用篾条铁丝圈住。这是打圈。如果新置盆桶，必须在作坊里做，这作坊就是箍桶店了。

Barrel Makers

Barrel makers carried their tools through the streets yelling “encircling” with hoarse voices, looking for residents that had pots, barrels and pans that needed repair. Household wood utensils would get loose as time went by, so they had to be “encircled” with bamboo strips or iron wires. New pot and barrels had to be made in the barrel workshop.

街坊修伞匠

旧时宁波城内外售伞、修伞成为一业。雨伞多以油纸或油布为伞面，竹子为伞骨。如果是布面钢骨的伞就是洋伞了。街头流动手工小摊的中老年人以修理雨伞为职业，挣些以几分钱计算的微薄收入以维持生计。

Neighborhood Umbrella Repair

In old Ningbo selling and repairing umbrellas was a common industry throughout the town. The umbrella uses oiled paper or oiled cloth to cover the bamboo ribs. Foreign umbrella are made of cloth and iron. The mid-aged and elderly men repaired umbrellas on the street with a mobile stall to earn a meager income.

编织草帽

宁波西乡的水田也种植细长的席草、编织凉帽、席子为业已有千年历史。草席、草帽编织以黄古林最为有名。草帽编好销往各地。由于编织属家庭副业，故曾有编户上万人，成为鄞西农民重要收入，现已刊为浙江省非物质文化遗产。

Woven Straw Hat

In the paddy fields Xixiang Ningbo slim mat grass is grown. The hat and mat making industry has existed for a thousand years. Huanggulin mats and hats are the most famous. Since it was a family sideline in old times, there were tens of thousands of households involved in it and it became the important income for farmers in Yinxi. Now it is identified as an intangible cultural heritage of Zhejiang.